ANNE GEDDES

motherhood

{ a journal }

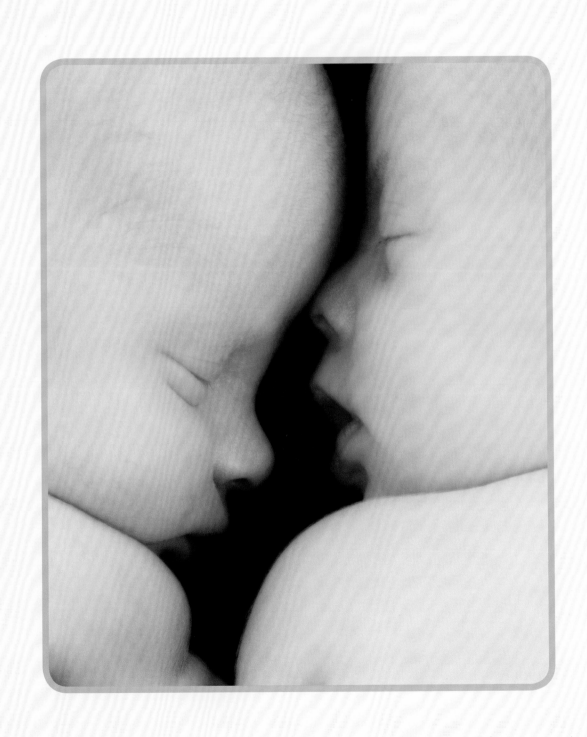

motherhood

{ a journal }

to _____

from _____

date _____

"Children are not only our hope for the future. By their very existence, they will be our future. And yet we so often take them for granted, or underestimate their essential importance. We need to take care of them now, educate, nurture and love them now, teach them the values of harmony, love, understanding, tolerance and an appreciation of other cultures now. Because now is the time to lay the right foundations for their future."

Anne Geddes

contents

{ all about me }

a mother's story

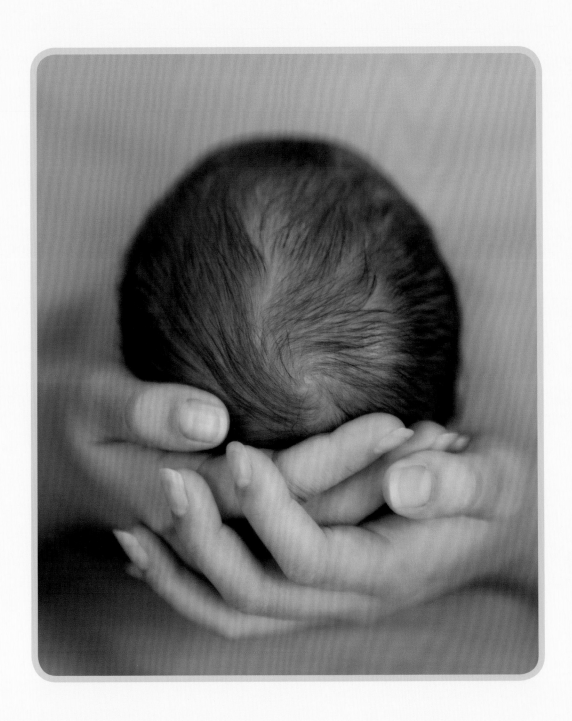

inspiration

This section is for your personal biography — a place to record details and memories of your own life and a chance to share your story with the next generation. Below are some ideas that you can use for direction and inspiration:

dearest friends

name

hopes & dreams

place & date of birth

important people
in my life

my mother's story

family tree

family history

people who have
influenced me

school

growing up

meeting the father
of my child

falling in love

medical history

likes & dislikes

my grandmother's story

faith & beliefs

passions

special moments

achievements

about me

{ a mother's story }

my photograph

family history

_____

_____

_____

_____

_____

_____

_____

_____

_____

_____

_____

_____

_____

_____

_____

_____

_____

_____

{ a mother's story }
family tree

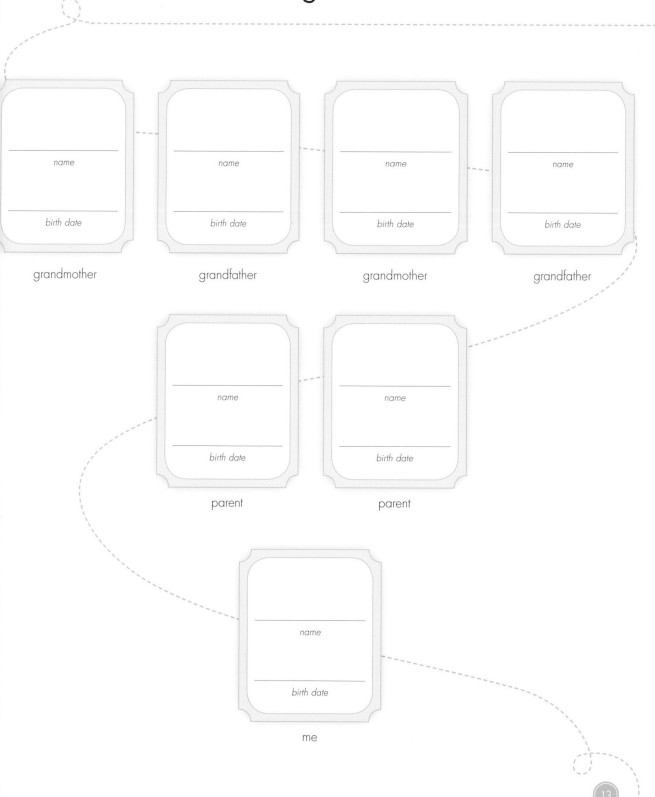

grandmother

grandfather

grandmother

grandfather

parent

parent

me

13

growing up

memories

memories

photographs

photographs

memories

_____

_____

_____

_____

_____

_____

_____

_____

_____

_____

_____

_____

_____

_____

_____

_____

_____

family & friends

_____
_____
_____
_____
_____
_____
_____
_____
_____
_____
_____
_____
_____
_____
_____
_____
_____
_____
_____

photographs

"Dance with your children,

be silly with them,

make mistakes and allow

yourself to be human

occasionally.

They'll love you for it."

{ anne geddes from her autobiography

A Labor of Love }

unconditional
love

{ memories of motherhood }

inspiration

This section is for you to record your memories of motherhood – the arrival of a new baby, milestones, quotes and precious moments to remember and to share. Below are some ideas for filling out the following pages:

❋ **My baby:** a place to record name, date of birth, weight and first memories of each of your children.

❋ **Milestones:** document the achievements and landmark occasions in the lives of your children.

❋ **Moments in time:** capture those precious moments which are significant to you as a mother – it could be a special occasion, a family vacation, a favorite place or simply a moment in time that, for you, represents the wonder of motherhood and family.

We have also left some blank pages for you to fill with other important memories of motherhood – to inspire you some ideas are:

quotes from my child

mother's day memories

when I look at you
I see ...

my definition of love

unconditional love

favorite memories of you

I understood motherhood
when ...

my definition of
motherhood

birthdays & vacations

what family means to me

my baby

{ unconditional love }

photographs

milestones

milestones

photographs

moments in time

{ photographs }

Time & Date _____

Place _____

Memory _____

_____

_____

_____

_____

_____

moments in time

{ photographs }

Time & Date _____

Place _____

Memory _____

_____

_____

_____

_____

_____

moments in time

{ photographs }

Time & Date

Place

Memory

moments in time

{ photographs }

Time & Date _____

Place _____

Memory _____

_____

_____

_____

_____

moments in time

{ photographs }

Time & Date _____

Place _____

Memory _____

_____

_____

_____

_____

_____

moments in time

{ photographs }

Time & Date _____

Place _____

Memory _____

_____

_____

_____

_____

memories of motherhood

_____

_____

_____

_____

_____

_____

_____

_____

_____

_____

_____

_____

_____

_____

_____

_____

_____

memories of motherhood

photographs

photographs

memories of motherhood

"Babies are our future –

so pure, so perfect, so innocent and

with so much promise."

{ anne geddes from her autobiography

A Labor of Love }

pearls of
wisdom

{ thoughts I'd like to share }

inspiration

This section is for your very own pearls of wisdom – advice, wishes and dreams,

personal inspiration and a special place for you to write letters to your children.

Below are some ideas that may help you fill the following pages:

my wishes & dreams for
you my child

my best advice for life

my heroes

famous family recipes

words of wisdom from my
mother

I understood motherhood
when ...

my inspiration
(book – movie – song)

I trust you because ...

our family traditions

thoughts I'd like to share

thoughts I'd like to share

photographs

a letter to my child

Date _____

Dear _____

_____

_____

_____

_____

_____

_____

_____

_____

_____

_____

_____

_____

_____

_____

a letter to my child

Date _____

Dear _____

_____

_____

_____

_____

_____

_____

_____

_____

_____

_____

_____

_____

_____

_____

a letter to my child

Date _____

Dear _____

_____

_____

_____

_____

_____

_____

_____

_____

_____

_____

_____

_____

_____

a letter to my child

Date _____

Dear _____

_____

_____

_____

_____

_____

_____

_____

_____

_____

_____

_____

_____

_____

_____

_____

my inspiration

hopes & dreams

the meaning of life

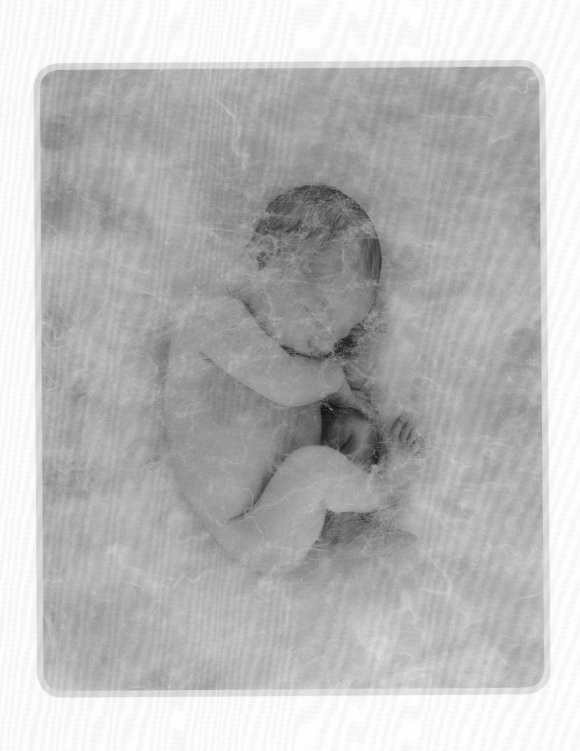

"Babies are
love made visible."

{ american proverb }

a mother's legacy

{ my gift to you }

inspiration

This section is especially reserved for you to record those personal details that you may wish to share with your children when they reach a certain milestone age or simply when the time feels right. Below are some ideas to help you:

what you mean to me

a message for my child

I'll tell you a secret

the important people

things you should
never forget

all the answers

motherhood & family

you are my inspiration

I always wanted to
tell you ...

I love you because ...

you'll always be my baby

you are so special

my definition of life

my legacy

final thoughts

i'll tell you a secret

my gift to you

my gift to you

photographs

{ a mother's legacy }

what you mean to me

photographs

I want you to know

I want you to know

my legacy

{ a mother's legacy }

photographs

final thoughts

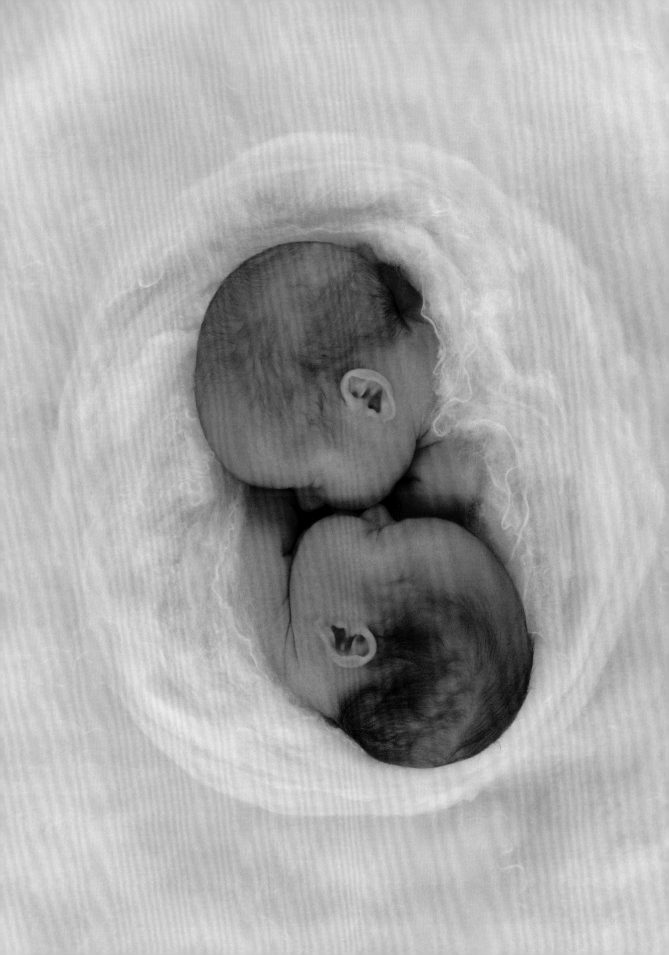

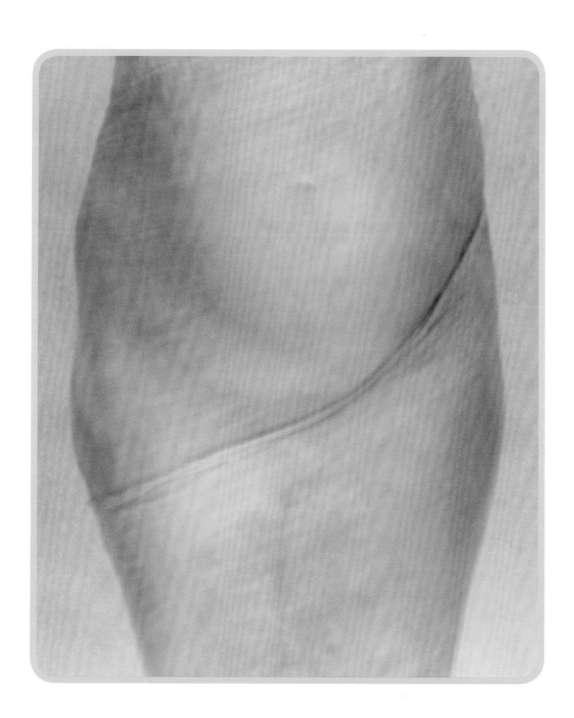

family
is forever

{ all the important people }

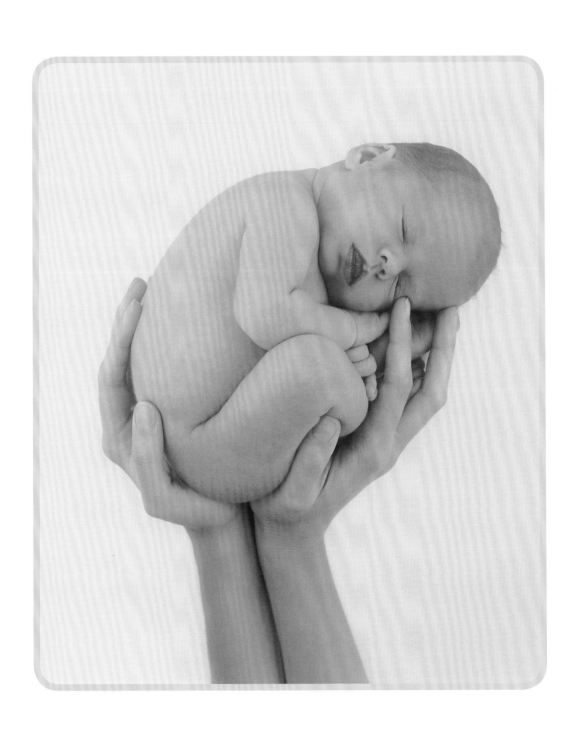

all the important people

This section is for you to record the details of all those important friends and family members in your life who will remain in the lives of your children. Note contact details, birth dates, star signs, wedding anniversaries, your relationship to them ... this is your personal record of significant people!

grandparents

godparents

cousins

dearest friends

brothers & sisters

family advisor

nieces & nephews

aunts & uncles

all the important people

name: _____

address: _____

_____

phone: _____

email: _____

birthday: _____

anniversaries: _____

notes: _____

_____

_____

name: _____

address: _____

_____

phone: _____

email: _____

birthday: _____

anniversaries: _____

notes: _____

_____

_____

name: _____

address: _____

_____

phone: _____

email: _____

birthday: _____

anniversaries: _____

notes: _____

_____

_____

name: _____

address: _____

_____

phone: _____

email: _____

birthday: _____

anniversaries: _____

notes: _____

_____

_____

{ family is forever }

all the important people

name:

address:

phone:

email:

birthday:

anniversaries:

notes:

name:

address:

phone:

email:

birthday:

anniversaries:

notes:

name: _____

address: _____

_____

phone: _____

email: _____

birthday: _____

anniversaries: _____

notes: _____

_____

_____

name: _____

address: _____

_____

phone: _____

email: _____

birthday: _____

anniversaries: _____

notes: _____

_____

_____

all the important people

name:

address:

phone:

email:

birthday:

anniversaries:

notes:

name:

address:

phone:

email:

birthday:

anniversaries:

notes:

name:

address:

phone:

email:

birthday:

anniversaries:

notes:

name:

address:

phone:

email:

birthday:

anniversaries:

notes:

all the important people

name: _____

address: _____

_____

phone: _____

email: _____

birthday: _____

anniversaries: _____

notes: _____

_____

_____

name: _____

address: _____

_____

phone: _____

email: _____

birthday: _____

anniversaries: _____

notes: _____

_____

_____

name: _____

address: _____

_____

phone: _____

email: _____

birthday: _____

anniversaries: _____

notes: _____

_____

_____

name: _____

address: _____

_____

phone: _____

email: _____

birthday: _____

anniversaries: _____

notes: _____

_____

_____

notes

{ family is forever }

photographs

{ family is forever }

photographs

notes

{ family is forever }

notes

_____

_____

_____

_____

_____

_____

_____

_____

_____

_____

_____

_____

_____

_____

_____

_____

_____

photographs

"The family is one
of nature's
masterpieces."

{ george santayana (1863-1952) }

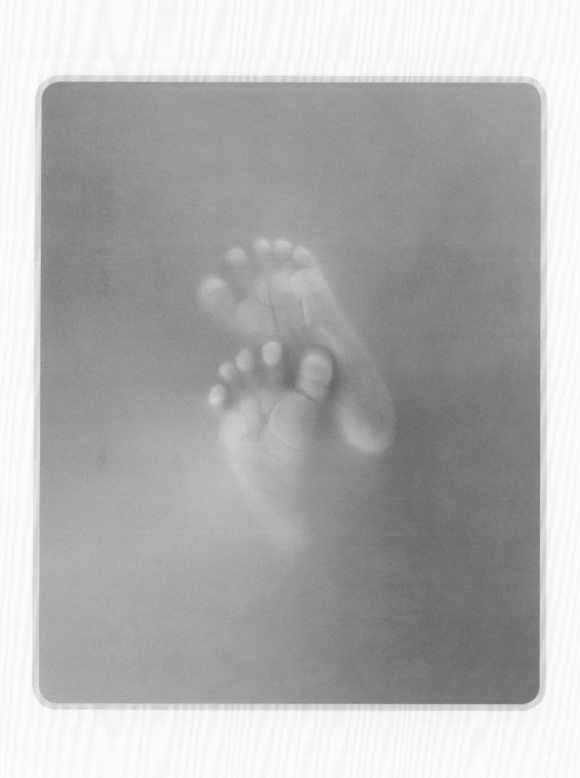

ANNE GEDDES ®

www.annegeddes.com

ISBN: 978-1-921652-16-5 - Emma with Matthew Cover
ISBN: 978-1-921652-23-3 - Emily with Talia Cover

First published in 2009 by Anne Geddes Publishing
Geddes Group Holdings Pty Ltd
Registered Office
Level 9, 225 George Street,
Sydney 2000, Australia

12 11 10 9 8 7 6 5 4 3 2 1

Designed by Kirsten Bryce
Produced by Kel Geddes
Printed in China by 1010 Printing International Limited, Hong Kong